KIRBY HALL

NORTHAMPTONS

Lucy Worsley

Inspector of Ancient Monuments and Historic Buildings

Kirby Hall was begun in 1570 by Sir Humphrey Stafford but completed by Sir Christopher Hatton, one of Queen Elizabeth I's favourite courtiers. It was one of many great Elizabethan houses built in the hope of receiving the queen on her annual 'progresses' around the country. While Kirby is smaller than some of the other houses, its richly carved decoration is exceptional and shows the arrival in England of new ideas in architecture and design. Ambition lay behind the building of Kirby Hall, for the best rooms of the house were reserved for royal visitors. Sir Christopher Hatton's descendants made improvements to the house and particularly to the gardens, once described as 'ye finest in England'. After the death of the fourth Christopher Hatton in 1706, however, the house was occupied less often and in the nineteenth century fell into ruin. After the Hall came into the guardianship of English Heritage, an important excavation in the gardens in 1987–94 resulted in the reconstruction of the Great Garden of the 1690s.

❖ CONTENTS ❖

Published by English Heritage, 1 Waterhouse Square, 138–142 Holborn, London EC1N 2ST
© English Heritage 2000 First published by English Heritage 2000, reprinted 2003, 2005, 2006
Photographs by English Heritage Photographic Unit and copyright
of English Heritage, unless otherwise stated.
Visit our website at www.english-heritage.org.uk
Edited by Kate Jeffrey and Sarah Yates
Designed by Pauline Hull. Plans and line drawings by Hardlines
Printed in England by the colourhouse, London
C40 12/06 07564 ISBN 1 85074 747 4

TOUR OF KIRBY HALL

Go along the path from the shop through the gateway into the forecourt.

Forecourt

The forecourt, where important visitors were met, provides a fitting formal framework for the grand entrance front of the house. The two large gateways to your left and right were built by Sir Christopher Hatton (I) and are similar to another pair at Holdenby, his main house in Northamptonshire. The entrance to the house had originally been through the east gate, from the

Above: The gateway by Nicholas Stone in the north wall of the forecourt. It originally stood in the West Garden

Left: View across the forecourt to the north front of the Hall

© CROWN COPYRIGHT.NMR

public road running alongside the east wall of the house. The smaller gate in the north wall through which you entered is in the fashionable Classical style of the leading mason Nicholas Stone, who worked at Kirby in 1638–40 for Sir Christopher Hatton (III). It stood in the south wall of the garden but was moved to the forecourt in 1693 when the gardens were remodelled (see pp16–21). The arcading along the top of the wall also came from the garden.

In the 1690s avenues of trees were planted to run east and north from the forecourt. The later western drive, now the approach to the house, is lined by chestnut trees planted by the Northamptonshire Girl Guides' Association in 1935 to commemorate the Silver Jubilee of George V.

North front

Originally, the north front of the house facing you had the common Elizabethan combination of a gateway tower and a turret at each corner, similar to that at Burghley House, Cambridgeshire, completed in 1587 for William Cecil, Lord Burghley, one of Elizabeth I's principal advisors. Later, the gaps between the towers were filled in with staircases, and in the late 1630s several features – the balustrades, round-headed windows, iron balcony and decorative curved gables – were added by Stone in the most up-to-date architectural style, copying ideas from the court architect Inigo Jones. Stone had worked as master-mason for Jones on such well-known buildings as James I's Banqueting House (completed 1622)

Development of the north front: (top) when first built in 1570; (centre) alterations afer 1575; (bottom) remodelling by Nicholas Stone in 1638–40 (reconstruction from J Heward and R Taylor, The Country House of Northamptonshire, *1996)*

Right: Engraving (c. 1700) of the Banqueting House, Whitehall, London, by Inigo Jones. A row of windows with similar alternate curved and triangular pediments formed part of Stone's work in the inner courtyard at Kirby

The BANQUETING HOUSE.

ARCHITECTURAL PATTERN BOOKS

In the sixteenth and seventeenth centuries the revival of interest in ancient Greek and Roman art had a considerable impact on architecture. These new influences appeared in English architecture via 'pattern books', or books of ornamental designs for masons. It seems that at Kirby someone with an educated interest in architecture provided the masons with various pattern books from which they copied.

In the courtyard the narrow band of wave motifs around the top of the walls, the star pattern under the entrance arch and the decorative capitals flanking the entrance are copied directly from the Italian architect Sebastiano Serlio's *Fourth Book of Architecture* (1537). *The First and Chief Grounds of Architecture* (1563) by the Englishman John Shute was used for the panels on each side of the entrance. However, the design is taken from the title-page of Shute's book, not the illustrations themselves, showing the masons' creative approach. One possible source for the giant pilasters around the courtyard was the French architect Philibert de l'Orme's *Architecture* (1567).

Left: Detail of one of the richly carved panels in the inner courtyard

Right: Title-page of John Shute's First and Chief Grounds of Architecture

in Whitehall, London. In fact, for many years it was thought that Jones had been involved here. Hatton (III) would have been familiar with Stone's work through his visits to London and service at court.

The square heads of the earlier windows can still be seen above the curved heads of the later ground-floor windows, especially on the right hand side. The workmanship of these changes in 1638–40 was not very neat; the sides of the original windows have been left in place but grooved to resemble the construction of the rest of the wall.

The bust of Apollo *above the central windows on the north side of the inner courtyard. The window is dated 1638*

The north side of the inner courtyard, *showing the innovative giant pilasters*

Go straight ahead into the inner courtyard. Turn around to look at the loggia.

Loggia and inner courtyard

This combination of an arcade, or loggia, behind a gatehouse was typically French, but despite its cosmopolitan style, the loggia was known to the household by the old-fashioned term of the 'cloister'. In the sixteenth century the arcade supported a long gallery at first-floor level, reached by staircases at either end. This gallery, used until a new long gallery was created in the west wing to overlook the gardens, had large rectangular windows, traces of

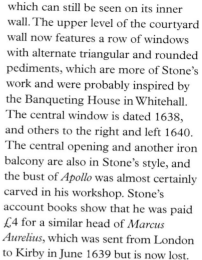

which can still be seen on its inner wall. The upper level of the courtyard wall now features a row of windows with alternate triangular and rounded pediments, which are more of Stone's work and were probably inspired by the Banqueting House in Whitehall. The central window is dated 1638, and others to the right and left 1640. The central opening and another iron balcony are also in Stone's style, and the bust of *Apollo* was almost certainly carved in his workshop. Stone's account books show that he was paid £4 for a similar head of *Marcus Aurelius*, which was sent from London to Kirby in June 1639 but is now lost.

The decoration of the courtyard is one of the most innovative features of Kirby Hall. Around all four sides run pilasters, or columns applied to the wall. They run through both floors of the building and are therefore called giant pilasters. While small Classical columns had been used to decorate buildings in England before the late sixteenth century, this courtyard is the first example of such details being used to unite the design of a whole façade.

Despite this innovative decoration, the main range opposite the loggia is traditional in plan. In a medieval manor the range housing the hall and service rooms was essentially asymmetrical. The great hall was entered by turning right from a passage that ran across the width of the range; doors on the left of the passage led to the service rooms.

But here the same arrangement has been disguised to look symmetrical. Left of the porch, the large windows concealed two separate floors of service rooms, and to the right, the windows rise through the double height of the hall. The window at the extreme right breaks forward and is longer than the others because it provided extra light to the high table for the lord at the end of the hall. It is balanced visually in the left-hand corner by another long window, which has no practical purpose.

This effort towards symmetry – which can be seen even as you enter the forecourt – reveals a whole new attitude towards building, signalling that the Renaissance ideas of proportion and balance, derived from Classical architecture, had arrived in England. However, Kirby Hall is not quite perfectly symmetrical, as its plan shows that the courtyard does not have right-angled corners. This is probably because it was built from the remains of an earlier house, traces of which survive in the area to the left of the porch.

East and west lodgings

The eight doors around the courtyard led to sets of lodgings for the family and servants. A house like Kirby was home to perhaps forty or fifty people when the owner was in residence. The whole household, organised hierarchically, was known as the 'family', but only some of the more

important members were the owner's blood-relations. They considered it a privilege to serve him. These upper servants would have had their own suites of rooms, entered through these doors, and would have crossed the courtyard to wait on the owner in his suite. The door in the far right-hand corner, closest to the 'high table' end of the hall, is slightly larger than the others and probably led to the suite of Sir Humphrey Stafford himself. The doors are decorated with fine carving of foliage and emblems. One of the symbols often repeated is a knot, the emblem or badge of the Stafford family, and on

The main range on the south side of the courtyard – the service rooms were on the left of the porch, and the Great Hall on the right

The remains of the west range today

Left: Part of the beautifully carved frieze around the inner courtyard

*Top row: the initials HS
and MS, of Sir Humphrey
Stafford's parents, above
one of the courtyard doors,
and the Stafford family's
coat of arms in the centre
Bottom row: the panels with
Sir Humphrey Stafford's
motto and the date 1572
on the porch*

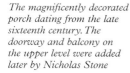

*The magnificently decorated
porch dating from the late
sixteenth century. The
doorway and balcony on
the upper level were added
later by Nicholas Stone*

the west side one doorway features the initials HS and MS of Sir Humphrey's parents.

The first floor of the west wing was taken up by the Long Gallery. An inventory from 1619 tells us that there were then four bedrooms on its ground floor, each with a 'pallet chamber' where the personal servants of the bedrooms' occupants would sleep on low beds, or pallets. Sir Christopher Hatton (II) and his wife, Alice, each had a bedroom and a 'pallet room' here and, in addition, a closet: a small, intimate room for private activities such as writing or conversation. Lady Hatton also had a bathing chamber. Although baths were taken extremely rarely at this time, she had two bathing tubs, according to the 1619 inventory.

Porch

The porch is one of the most exuberant displays of architectural ornament to be found in England and is typical of the Thorpe family of masons, the probable builders of the Hall, who used French pattern books as their source. The features of the lower two floors, such as the

Classical pilasters, are relatively common, although here very finely carved, but the curved top gable, with its nine tiny columns with Corinthian capitals, is almost unique. Stafford's responsibility for this part of the building is clear: his knot and motto *Ie seray loyal* (I will be loyal).

Humphrey Stafford's name as shown in two panels above the hall windows; (centre) the Stafford knot, a badge of the family; (far left and right) a badge of a related family, and the Stafford crest

appear on the porch, and its gable is dated 1572. His name, HVMFRE STAFARD, is carved on two panels above the hall windows, and the dates 1572 and 1575 appear above the two projecting windows. As the first stone was laid in 1570, this range must have taken five years to build.

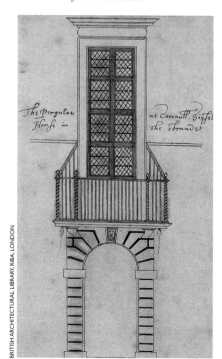

British Architectural Library, RIBA, London

The doorway and balcony at first floor level, dated 1638, were added to the porch by Stone. The combination of doorway and balcony was known as a 'pergola', and an early example from a house in the Strand, London, was drawn in 1618 by John Smythson, another mason/designer. Inside the porch, the plaster ceiling is one of the later seventeenth-century additions in a fleshier style than Stone's work. It features the initials CH (for Christopher Hatton) and the Hatton crest of the hind around the edge. The explorer Sir Francis Drake named his ship the *Golden Hinde* because the first Sir Christopher financed his voyages.

Go under the porch and into the Great Hall.

Great Hall

The Great Hall has been greatly altered since the sixteenth century, but it is still possible to see that it was based firmly on a medieval plan. The door from the porch originally opened into a narrow corridor, called the screens passage, with a large, carved wooden screen standing to

The ornate plasterwork ceiling inside the porch, added in the later seventeenth century

Left: A 'pergola' drawn by John Smythson in 1618, showing an iron railing similar to that on Stone's new porch balcony

The east end of the Great Hall, showing the ceiling restored to its original colour

the right with openings through to the hall beyond. In the stone wall to the left there were once two doors leading to the service rooms. Above the passage there might have been a minstrels' gallery. Turning right and passing through the screen, visitors would have been faced with rows of long tables, where the household ate, and a large table across the end of the hall, lit by the extra long window, which was traditionally for the lord.

The hall was originally better lit, for the outlines of two large blocked windows can be seen on either side of the fireplace. The original unpainted oak ribs and blue panels of the ceiling were retained until the nineteenth

century, and have now been reinstated. The room lost many features in three main periods of alteration. The first was 1638–40 when Nicholas Stone was employed to construct the round-headed door from the porch, and the one opposite that leads down steps into the private garden. Nineteenth-century guides to the house often called these the 'Queen's Steps' and say that Hatton (I) helped Elizabeth I down them, but there is no evidence that she ever visited Kirby.

In the 1670s Frances, Lady Hatton, redecorated the house while her husband, Sir Christopher Hatton (IV), was away. In one letter of 1678 she says that 'we dine in the hall

DINING IN THE SEVENTEENTH CENTURY

The household received their 'dyett' or meals as part of their remuneration and sat at carefully differentiated tables according to their rank. Accounts from the Hatton archives show that the owner ate white bread while his servants ate inferior brown 'household' bread. The owner's immediate relations were treated to exotic items such as sugar (which had to be sent from London), cinnamon, cloves, pepper and currants. Their main meal was over by 3 o'clock in the afternoon, and in the evening supper was served. The more important members of the household would not eat in the

hall every day. They used the Great Chamber for entertaining guests and even withdrew to their own parlour or eating room, if, for example, the weather was too cold. The retreat from the Great Hall may have been more convenient for the lord but was not always popular with his household. John Selden complained in the 1650s that 'the Hall was the place where the great Lord did used to eat ... where he saw all his servants and tenants about him. He eats not in private ... except in times of sickness; when once he became a thing cooped up, all his greatness was spoiled'.

The Great Hall, as it might have appeared in 1619, when an inventory of the house was made. Reconstruction drawing by Ivan Lapper

every day. I have hanged [sic] up the pictures and it looks very fine'. Surviving features from this period probably include the doorcase in the wall at the west end of the hall; this was originally balanced by a 'blind' door for the sake of symmetry. At roughly this period, the wooden screen was removed and the minstrels' gallery converted to a balcony, which gave access to the little room over the porch. The two doors to the offices were replaced with a single central one, and the whole wall panelled. The panelling was still in place at the turn of the twentieth century.

The last period of alteration was the 1960s, when the Ministry of Works decided to remove all later additions in order to show the house as it may have appeared when it was built. However, some alterations are very difficult, if not impossible, to reverse. For example, the outline of the central opening in the wall that remained after the removal of the panelling would not have existed in the sixteenth century. Before these changes the Great Hall had been a rare example of a hall that had survived from the late seventeenth century without any eighteenth-century or Victorian alterations.

The Great Stair

Right: The Long Gallery at Chastleton House, Oxfordshire, which also has a seventeenth-century barrel-vaulted plasterwork ceiling

Reconstruction drawing by Ivan Lapper of the Long Gallery at Kirby as it may have looked when complete

Go through the door at the west end of the Great Hall into the lobby.

Lobby and Great Stair

Important visitors would pass along the hall into the lobby, or 'staires foote', which features impressive stone door surrounds incorporating upturned obelisk motifs, and up the stairs to the Great Chamber above. The lobby contained an 'oyster table' in 1619; this was a table veneered with thin slices of laburnum wood with a pattern resembling oyster shells.

The stairs in a house intended to impress visitors, like this one, were very important. In 1579 Lord Burghley wrote of Hatton (I)'s Holdenby that he thought 'nothing of greater grace than your stately ascent from your hall to your great chamber, and your chamber answerable with largeness and lightsomeness'. Kirby

Hall was not on the same scale as Holdenby, but the spacious stairs, with a stone handrail fitted into the wall in the 1580s, rise up to another large lobby, or 'staires head'.

Go up the Great Stair.

Long Gallery

In a sixteenth-century house the most important rooms were hall, stair, great chamber, withdrawing room and long gallery. The gallery was usually the last in the sequence, but at Kirby you pass the end of it (to your left) before going into the Great Chamber. It took up the whole first floor of the west wing and originally had a barrel-shaped ceiling with plaster decoration, of which a small part survives over the 'staires head', added in the mid-seventeenth century; the walls were panelled.

The gallery was not just a place for walking during wet weather and for admiring the gardens. A little aside from the main hierarchical sequence of rooms, it could be used as neutral ground for members of

the household of different status to do business together; in the 1660s at Welbeck Abbey, Nottinghamshire, for example, the gallery was used by the Duke of Newcastle to call meetings of the workers and tenants from his outlying estates.

Turn right into the Great Chamber.

Great Chamber

The room to the right of the head of the stair was the Great Chamber, where important visitors were received, dinner was eaten on feast days, and entertainments such as music and masques were performed.

This room has been extensively altered since the sixteenth century. First came the addition of an extra window, in the far left-hand corner from the entrance, which looked over the private garden below. The window area has been blocked off with a flimsy partition, because the later Hattons wanted to regularise the shape of the room. In 1660 the entrance door was moved into the centre of the wall from its original position slightly further to the west. These changes were all aimed at emphasising the symmetry of the rooms.

In the eighteenth century the Finch-Hattons added a coved ceiling and a screen of columns, and used the room for balls. The square outlines of the column bases can be seen in the floor by the entrance. These later additions were removed in the 1960s,

THE GREAT CHAMBER ❖

The 1619 inventory tells us how the Great Chamber was used. Many visitors were expected, as there were no less than thirty-three seats. Valuable carpets were listed, but they would have been laid on the tables, not on the floor, which was matted. There were three great curtain rods for the hangings that would be put up when the Hattons came into residence. The images on the hangings told the story of Hercules. The sizes of the hangings are given, and match the combined length of the east and south walls where they must have hung.

The High Great Chamber at Hardwick Hall, Derbyshire. The hangings at Kirby must have been similarly sumptuous and colourful

NATIONAL TRUST PHOTOGRAPHIC LIBRARY/ANDREAS VON EINSIEDEL

but, again, the room could not be returned to its original layout, for the row of windows in the west wall are also alterations. The fireplace, dating from the seventeenth century, was brought here from Rufford Abbey in the twentieth century.

Lobby

Passing beyond the Great Chamber you enter the suite of more private rooms that Hatton (I) added so that they could be turned over to an important guest such as the queen; this suite was reserved for visitors while the family lived in the wings. The suite was not 'private' in the modern sense, for household members or guests of high status could be invited even into the bedchamber. People waited in the lobby before being summoned into the Great Withdrawing Chamber beyond, feeling privileged at having penetrated this far along the hierarchical sequence of rooms. Perhaps waiting on James I during his visit to Kirby in 1619, visitors could have admired the room's six pictures, 'where of 2 of them are the Knights of the Golden Fleece, the others of the frenche kings'.

Reconstruction drawing by Ivan Lapper of the Best Bedchamber, furnished according to the 1619 inventory

Great Withdrawing Chamber

When James I visited Kirby, he probably sat receiving compliments in this room on the cushions of cloth of silver starred with gold, on a chair under the canopy of white taffeta with purple and gold stars, that are listed in the 1619 inventory. Meanwhile, his courtiers could have entertained themselves playing billiards, as a billiard table, four balls and two ivory billiard sticks are also listed. Today, the room contains an elegant apse,

echoing the bay window opposite, and a delicate cornice, both late eighteenth-century insertions.

Best Bedchamber

The next room, also with a bay window, was described in 1619 as 'the best bedchamber'. While an important visitor would sleep here, bedchambers were also used for private day-time activities such as reading, as well as for receiving intimate or important guests. This was the most expensively furnished room in the house, containing a valuable looking-glass (mirror) with a cover inlaid in mother-of-pearl, as well as rare Persian carpets. The gilt bedstead was topped with four large gold balls and had curtains of crimson taffeta laced and fringed with gold. The hangings told the story of the Roman general Scipio's defeat of Hannibal, general of Carthage. The panelling and doorcases are eighteenth-century survivals, with the brown colour scheme reinstated.

Go down the secondary stair. At the bottom pass through a doorway opposite and slightly to your left into the Pallet Chamber.

Secondary stair and Pallet Chamber

The secondary stair, narrower than the Great Stair, would have been used by servants and intimate friends of the guest in the Best Bedchamber.

The ground floor of the state suite was lowered in the seventeenth century by about 30cm (12ins), which explains the odd position of the old handrail, left from the earlier, shorter stair when the staircase was lengthened. In the chamber at the foot of the stair, the doorway straight ahead enters a passage to the Great Hall, which was added to provide direct access to the more private rooms of the state suite. The personal servants of the occupants of the bedchambers beyond would have slept in this room, guarding the door. There was a further 'pallet chamber' in the attic and another in the cellar below for overspill.

Bedchambers / Billiard Room and Library

Turning right, you pass through two further rooms that were originally bedchambers, with bay windows like those above. The first had soft furnishings dominated by 'murrey sattin laced with gould lace' in 1619, and was later known as the Billiard Room. In the eighteenth century it was wall-papered, and above the window a 'pulley-board' for raising festoon curtains can still be seen. Fragments of the late eighteenth-century wallpaper, with a green *fleur de lys* pattern, have survived.

The next room was refitted as the Library about 1800, with bookshelves that blocked the windows overlooking the garden. The late seventeenth century panelling and doors survived these alterations, but were painted pale cream. As you leave by the corridor, you pass a tiny closet that once contained a close-stool or toilet, comprising a pewter 'stool pan' with a black leather cover.

Great Parlour and garden exhibition

Following the passage, you will see the doorway leading out into the garden, but first return to the Pallet Chamber. Turn left into the Great Parlour, which contains the exhibition about the gardens. Much altered, this room, originally used for informal dining, played a pivotal role in the design of the gardens. The middle window, looking along the central path, was once an enormous bay window like those in the state suite. The whole garden could be seen from this bay, which was later demolished and made into a door and then changed again into a small window. Something of the relationship between the house and garden was lost, for the spreading symmetry of the garden was intended to be appreciated from this point.

After looking at the exhibition, return past the bottom of the secondary stair to the doorway to the garden.

The smaller secondary stair. The stone handrail, which is now too high, dates from the late sixteenth century, before the staircase was lengthened.

The bay window in one of the ground-floor bedchambers, with a 'pulley-board' for raising festoon curtains above the window

THE WEST GARDEN

The West Garden at Kirby existed by the 1580s, when it appears on Ralph Treswell's surveys with the earliest images of the new house (see p25). These show an irregular enclosure labelled 'garden and orchard', which was probably remodelled in the early seventeenth century into a relatively plain design with raised terraces. What you see today is a recreation of its appearance in the 1690s, when Sir Christopher Hatton (IV) transformed it into 'ye finest garden in England'.

One of the gateways at the Botanic Gardens, Oxford, also designed by Stone

The Jacobean Garden

The early seventeenth-century garden at Kirby Hall and the new one made in the 1690s were quite different from each other, but both were typical of many other gardens

© CROWN COPYRIGHT, NMR

of large houses across the country. The earlier garden was divided into four grass plots known as a 'parterre' (from the Latin *partire*, meaning 'to divide'). Excavations have shown that each quarter featured a statue and a scalloped edge bordered by a hedge. There was a raised terrace along two sides of the garden, supported by a brick wall, along the top of which ran the miniature arcade that can now be seen in the north wall of the forecourt. To the south was a free-standing brick wall.

The blind gateway that stands today in the northern terrace originally stood at the west end of the shorter walk, opposite the Great Parlour. It was remodelled by Nicholas Stone in 1638–40 to match his new gateway, set in the south garden wall. Both gateways were moved at the end of the seventeenth century, with the southern one taken to the forecourt (see p4). The style

This gateway by Nicholas Stone in the northern terrace was moved from its original position opposite the Great Parlour in the 1690s. The brick wall once entirely surrounded the West Garden

of the gateways is similar to those Stone built at the Oxford Botanic Gardens in 1621, a garden that is still enclosed within walls like Kirby was.

The Great Garden

In the late seventeenth century the garden was altered by Hatton (IV) with the help of his brother Charles Hatton, who was an expert plantsman. One interesting contract survives from 1683 when the gardener John Simpson was engaged. He was required to keep the garden in the same good order as he found it, providing his own tools, seeds, nails,

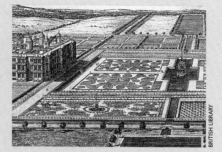

workmen and weeders. In return he received a salary, food for himself and one man, and the 'profits of fruits and other things ... over and above what is used in the house when his Lordship is there'.

Longleat House in Wiltshire also had a cutwork parterre laid out by the firm of London and Wise, shown immediately to the right of the house in this engraving by Kip and Knyff

BRITISH LIBRARY

The reconstructed parterre, with the west front of the Hall in the background

Mount

West Garden

West lodgings
and Long Gallery

Blind
gateway

Bay windows

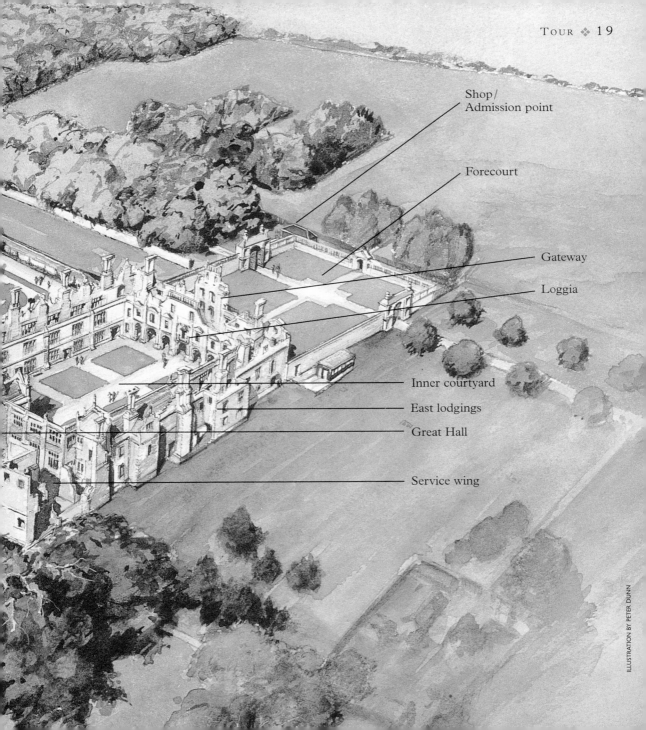

Shop/
Admission point

Forecourt

Gateway

Loggia

Inner courtyard

East lodgings

Great Hall

Service wing

ILLUSTRATION BY PETER DUNN

This design (c. 1685) for the parterre at Longleat House was adapted for the recreation of the parterre at Kirby. The notation corresponds to George London's arrangement of trees and shrubs in tubs, as reproduced at Kirby today

This urn, formerly from the Great Garden at Kirby, now survives in the garden of the nineteenth-century estate manager's house

A few years later, Simpson was overseeing works in the Great Garden, for which accounts survive dated 1685-6. The works included digging borders, bringing 'mould and dung', and laying out gravel paths.

The main remodelling was in the 1690s, when the western terrace was transformed into a grassy slope, extending out over the earlier path. An elaborate parterre in grass and gravel was created, similar to the one seen today. A design like this in the up-to-date court style of the gardens created by William III and Mary II could be laid out within weeks by using narrow bent wooden boards to divide gravelled areas from grass ones. Not enough evidence for the original pattern survived for it to be recreated, so the present reconstruction is adapted from a late seventeenth-century design made by the gardening firm London and Wise for Longleat House, Wiltshire.

George London probably advised on the Kirby design, for he visited Kirby in 1693 and agreed with Lady Hatton's suggestion that the garden's south brick wall should be pulled down. This opened up the view to a great formal plantation called a 'wilderness' (see plan on p30), stretching up the valley beyond the stream, which had been canalised to suit the more formal landscape.

The fragment of a statue depicting the *Rape of the Sabines* that lies at the west end of the shorter central walk is the only survivor of the many statues. The four sections of the garden were embellished with statues of Classical gods, including *Hercules* and *Mercury* (now lost), and decorative urns. They were probably similar to a set by Caius Gabriel Cibber from Belvoir Castle, made at about the same time. One of the urns still survives at a house in Gretton where the nineteenth-century estate manager lived.

Outside the garden to the south, a low hump marks the position of

❖ 'CHOICE EXOTICS' ❖

Charles Hatton wrote to his brother in 1694 that he had heard someone describe Hatton (IV) as having made Kirby 'ye finest garden in England'. This was probably not so much because of its design, although this was completely up-to-date, but because of the plants and seeds that Hatton (IV) had obtained, 'such things as are rare and may be picked up among the sea men'. Charles's letters mention his sending 'narcissus of Japan', 'some seeds of ye soape tree from China' and carob seeds that were to be raised in a pot set in a heated bed. Six apricot and six mulberry trees came from London in 1677, along with 'three score and ten white lilacs'. Three hundred almond trees were to be wiped of mould and buried in a cellar 'where ye frost would not come to prejudice them'. Rarer still were pomegranate trees and a 'Hyacinth of Peru'. Hatton (IV) seems to have loved his garden to the detriment of other business, as the House of Lords questioned his non-attendance in 1688, 1696 and 1704.

Top left: Eighteenth-century watercolour of Deep Purple Lilac by G. D. Ehret

Top right: Almond (c.1568) by Jacques Le Moyne de Morgues

Right: Pomegranate (c.1568) by Jacques Le Moyne de Morgues

the 'mount'. This was left behind deliberately to create a vantage point when the surrounding land was lowered to form a terrace down towads the stream. It was also the site of the church in the former village (see p25), and an eighteenth-century account recalls that when the graveyard was dug away, several cart-loads of bones were removed.

The remains of the 'mount' to the south of the West Garden

West front and bay windows

The west front, viewed from the West Garden, was originally long and low, punctuated only by chimneys. Hatton (I) added the decorative gables and the projecting stairtower that disrupts the regular visual rhythm of the chimneys. After the state suite was added, the whole southern end of the west front was refaced to regularise the windows. The hole for the old drain-pipe survives in the string course over one of the new windows, now in the wrong place, and the outlines of the earlier larger windows can still he seen in the walls of the Library.

One of the most striking features of Kirby Hall is the pair of bay windows at the end of the state suite. The writer Sacheverell Sitwell fancifully described them in 1945 as being 'set side by side, like two huge galleons tied up at anchor. They are like the poops of two stone ships, never meant to sail, but only to catch the sunlight, and their gables in fact are like the ships floating and reflected, keel uppermost'. Their curved shape distinguishes them from other late sixteenth-century windows, which tend to be polygonal with straight sides. The exterior of the house must have once been even more spectacular as there were two further bays: one in the Great Parlour on the west front, and one on the opposite side facing east. Only their foundations below ground survive. Outward-looking windows like this were revolutionary at a time when most people lived in houses facing into courtyards, primarily for defence.

Go down the steps at the south end of the garden and cross the lawn, past the bay windows, to reach the remains of the service wing.

Kirby Hall's most striking feature: the two surviving bay windows facing outwards from the state suite

Service wing

Passing round the bay windows and under the cedar tree, you cross what was probably the owner's 'privy' or private garden. To your left, beyond the Great Hall, is the service wing. It was supplemented by another, now missing range, the foundations of which were excavated south-east of the kitchen. The sequence of rooms in the service wing moving eastwards from the Great Hall is difficult to establish because little survives, but a plan of c.1670 shows a buttery and a 'little hall' with a fireplace. Beyond was a 'pastry' with bread-ovens and the kitchen to the south. The buttery took its name from its original use for storing butts of beer, supervised by a butler. In 1678 Frances Hatton begged her husband for 'some sort of genteel servant to be about the house for I have no creature but the Buttler'.

The kitchen chimney in the south-east corner retains the equipment for turning the spit. The stairtower contains a remarkable cantilevered staircase. As it lacks a balustrade it was probably never completed. It was probably added in the late seventeenth century, and led up to rooms with elaborate plaster ceilings.

From here you can return to the entrance by passing round the east front of the house to the east gateway or side gate into the forecourt.

The remains of the service wing

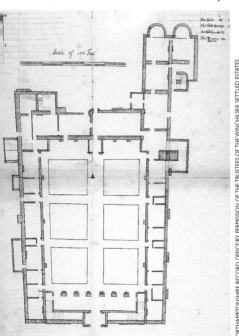

Scale of 100 Feet

Left: This survey of Kirby, probably dating from c. 1670, shows how the lodgings in the west range and rooms in the service wing were originally partitioned

A rare photograph of 1882 showing the elaborate plasterwork ceiling, now lost, from the cantilevered staircase in the south-east corner of the house

HISTORY

The early house

Sir Humphrey Stafford's father, also called Humphrey, came from Blatherwycke in Northamptonshire. In 1542 he acquired Kirby, which had previously been owned partly by Fineshade Priory in the north east of the county, and partly by the Brudenells of neighbouring Deene Park. In the documents of the property transfer he is called 'of Kirby', which suggests that there was a house before his son and heir began building. Three features of the service wing also suggest this: firstly, the south wall is on a slightly different alignment to that of the Great Hall. Secondly, there are remains of an early Tudor window in the cellar under the south-east staircase and, finally, the basement structure is so irregular that it was probably much earlier than the carefully planned work of Stafford.

Sir Humphrey Stafford

Sir Humphrey Stafford inherited Kirby in 1548. In 1566 he was appointed Sheriff of Northamptonshire and

The Stafford crest

probably began to feel the need for a larger and more fashionable house. In the previous year Elizabeth I had been on a 'progress' to Northamptonshire and had stayed in several houses nearby, including Deene Park. A dozen of Stafford's neighbours within twelve miles were building or had built great houses in the new style, with huge windows facing outwards, now that defence was no longer a priority in domestic building. The greatest were Sir William Cecil's house at Burghley and Sir Walter Mildmay's at Apethorpe.

Stafford's rebuilding of Kirby Hall began in 1570. Unusually, we know the exact year because a plan of the house survives, on which the surveyor John Thorpe wrote '*Kerby whereof I layd ye first stone AD 1570*'. This plan had been known since the eighteenth century, and it was therefore assumed until quite recently that John Thorpe had designed the house. However, in 1949, the architectural historian John Summerson pointed out that in 1570

❖ THE LOST MEDIEVAL VILLAGE ❖

Kirby Hall was built on the edge of a medieval village that has now almost completely disappeared. The name Kirby, probably of ninth-century origin, was derived from 'Cherchberie', meaning a village with a church. By 1086 the Domesday survey recorded that there were six householders in Kirby. In 1539 another survey indicated that there were ten able-bodied men in the village, and their houses are shown clearly in Treswell's surveys of 1586 and 1587. The village was already partially deserted, and the church and most of the rest of the houses were demolished during the making of the Jacobean Garden. The only visible traces of the village are the earthwork remains of the long street running up the slope on the other side of the brook. The nearest building was a large farm complex, whose outline can still be made out when the sun is low.

A survey of Kirby (1586) by Ralph Treswell. The triangular enclosure containing the church was later subsumed into the West Garden

Right: The sunken remains of the village street running uphill to the south-east of the Hall

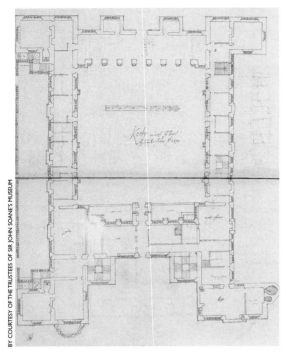

The famous plan for Kirby Hall made by the surveyor John Thorpe. His note in the centre reads 'Kerby whereof I layd ye first stone AD 1570'

John Thorpe was only about seven years old. He could still have laid the first stone because this was a ceremony often performed by children. It was probably his father, Thomas Thorpe, who came from a well-known family of masons from the nearby village of Kingscliffe, who actually oversaw the building.

The design of the house was often a collaborative effort by the patron, surveyor and masons without the involvement of an architect in the modern sense. Thorpe and the Kirby masons used an unusual Anglo-French style that can also be seen nearby in the porch of Dingley Hall (1558–60), in a monument in the church of Braybrooke (c.1570) and in a porch at Deene Park, only three miles away. However, Stafford's mark was firmly on the house for his name appears above the Great Hall windows, and his knot badge and his parents' initials appear over the doorways of the inner courtyard.

Sir Christopher Hatton (I) (1540-91)

Sir Christopher Hatton (I) bought Stafford's unfinished work in 1575 but rarely used Kirby and his several other houses. He shows how he intended his house at Holdenby to function in a letter of 1583, when he planned his first visit to Kirby, 'leaving my other shrine, I mean Holdenby, still unseen, until that holy saint may sit in it to whom it is dedicated'. His view of the queen as a saint, and his houses as her shrines, explains why the best rooms of a house could remain unoccupied by its owner and how the greatest visitors from court would expect to take over their host's house as their own. As Stafford's house had a great chamber above a parlour, but no formal suite, the rooms added to the south west of the house were probably the work of Hatton (I), who moved in the elevated circles where such apartments were essential. Kirby was not on the scale of vast Holdenby, but it did receive five royal visits in the early seventeenth century, after Hatton (I)'s debts had forced his descendants to sell Holdenby to the Crown. Important visitors still caused a stir in 1668, when Lady Hatton wrote to her son that her husband had not even been across the courtyard since his arrival from London, but on a day that a great courtier came, 'as soon as he heard ye coach was near, he himself went

❖ SIR CHRISTOPHER HATTON (I) ❖

The first Sir Christopher Hatton was a glamorous figure of the Elizabethan court, and made a meteoric rise to become Lord Chancellor and a Knight of the Garter. It is rumoured that he first caught the queen's eye by his excellent dancing. With his rapid promotions, his building of great houses and his death in debt, he was described by one contemporary as a 'mere vegetable of the court that sprung up at night and sank again at his noon'. His main house was at Holdenby, begun in 1571, of which only the kitchen quarters and two gateways, which flanked the forecourt, survive. At his nephew's wedding Hatton is said to have thrown off his robes of office, saying 'Lie thou there, chancellor', and joined in the dancing.

An unusual sixteenth-century portrait of Sir Christopher Hatton (I), possibly by Sir William Segar

to ye gate & caused ye great gates to be opened and stayed thereabouts near a quarter of an hour to wait their coming'.

Sir Christopher Hatton (II) (d.1619)

Hatton (I) died childless and in debt, and Kirby passed to his nephew William Newport, who took the name Hatton. Newport too was childless and, at his death, the Hall was inherited by Sir Christopher Hatton (II), a distant relation who had married Alice Fanshawe of Ware Park in Hertfordshire. He welcomed the queen, Anne of Denmark, to Kirby in August 1605 for three nights, and her husband, James I, visited in 1612, 1616, 1619 and

1624. An inventory survives that is almost certainly of Kirby Hall at the date of Hatton (II)'s death in 1619, giving the fullest picture of how the house was furnished in its heyday, when the king would have taken over the whole of the south-west wing, and the house would have been used as was originally intended. James I's last visit in 1624 was unfortunate, for a letter-writer in London wrote that he had heard little from the court's tour of Northamptonshire except that 'there be many sick of this spotted ague, which took away the Duke of Lennox in few days. He died at Kirby a house of young Hatton's'.

Sir Christopher Hatton (III) (1605-70)

The third Sir Christopher Hatton, who inherited in 1619, was a friend and patron of the antiquary Sir William Dugdale and built up a famous collection of old charters (published by the Northamptonshire Record Society). He ordered the improvements to the house carried out by Nicholas Stone in 1638–40. For his support of the royalist cause in the Civil War (1642–9) he was created Baron Hatton of Kirby in 1643. When the royalists were defeated, he was forced to flee to France. Although he was happy there with his 'books and fiddles', he found it difficult to claim his money and estates, and did not return home

Portrait (c. 1612) of Anne of Denmark attributed to Marcus Gheeraerts the Younger

Portrait (1621) of King James I by Daniel Mytens. James visited Kirby four times between 1612 and 1624

until 1656. In 1655 his wife Elizabeth wrote to him that she had arrived at Kirby '... and found all ye poor children well though stark naked Charles with only half a shirt ... if I can get any body to lend me a little money I must be forced to quite clothe them all'. Elizabeth was not used to skimping on her own clothing: like all those who appeared at court she displayed her wealth and status through her dress, and one of her bills survives for dressmaking materials such as 'sarcenet to line a bodice', a 'stomacher laces and ribbons' to tie round her waist, and buckram, bone and hooks to support the stiff ensembles.

The women of the Hatton family ran the house in the absence of their husbands, but Elizabeth seems to have lived in fear of Hatton (III). In one of her letters to her son of the 1660s, she admitted: 'I am afraid without your advice to speak to him of any business ... he desired that I would order ye affairs of ye house and take ye accounts' and, fearing his displeasure, she agreed. Hatton (III), meanwhile, was in London, amusing himself with the 'discourse of players and such idle people'. Cecelia, wife of their son Christopher Hatton (IV), also kept the household accounts and resolved disputes over unpaid bills. 'I have here in my book set down paid the lockmakers bill April ye 9, there is the lie disproved', she wrote on one occasion.

© CROWN COPYRIGHT: UK GOVERNMENT ART COLLECTION

Sir Christopher Hatton (IV) as a boy in 1641 by Cornelius Johnson

Sir Christopher Hatton (IV) (1632-1706)

In 1662 Hatton (III) was appointed governor of the island of Guernsey, which took him away from home again, but he failed to pay the garrison there and did not stay for long. The post was also filled, more successfully, by his son Christopher Hatton (IV), who inherited Kirby in 1670, but spent the next ten years in Guernsey. He was made Viscount Hatton of Gretton in 1683.

Elizabeth Hatton wrote to her son again from Kirby in 1670 that Cecelia 'complains of a pain in her head ... but to tell you really my thoughts her greatest trouble is for parting so long from you'. Sadly, shortly after Elizabeth and her daughter-in-law went to Guernsey to visit Hatton (IV), they were both killed in a terrible accident: the gunpowder magazine of the castle in which they were staying was struck by lightning and exploded. Hatton (IV)'s daughter Anne, however, was saved by his black servant James Chapple, who was rewarded with a pension and lived for fifty years in the village of Gretton. Hatton (IV) married twice more, but his second wife Frances was also abandoned when he returned to Guernsey and also found herself short of money. She was overseeing some redecorating and building works, but was unable to pay the workmen. 'I never walk out of doors but some of them meet me with bills so that I am afraid to go in the court', she wrote in 1677.

The most numerous letters in the Hatton archives are between Hatton

Right: Hyacinth and narcissi by J. J. Walther

(IV) and his brother Charles, often about plants for the Great Garden (see pp 16–21). Charles was a lively correspondent and, apparently, a lively personality. At Christmas 1667 he wrote complaining that he had not heard music for some time, and added 'you will thereby easily imagine how melancholy I have been considering how well I love dancing and how excellent I am at it'. As well as sending plants, Charles also carried out jobs for his brother in London such as getting portraits from Kirby cleaned.

The diarist John Evelyn, visiting in 1654, had found Kirby Hall pleasant but the 'seat naked' and the 'avenue ungraceful'. However, in the late seventeenth century the whole estate was made more formal with avenues of trees, and the stream made into a canal. In 1697 Charles wrote that the northerly new riding lined with horse chestnut trees must mean that distant Gretton was almost visible from the wilderness. Despite all these efforts, Kirby's glory did not

This reconstruction drawing of the plantations and wilderness at Kirby Hall c. 1700 is based on an eighteenth-century plan of the Brudenell family's estate, which adjoins Kirby to the south

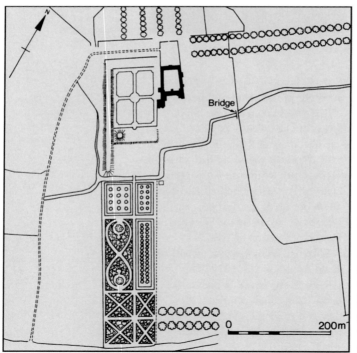

Bridge

0   200m

❖ GARDEN ARCHAEOLOGY ❖

One interesting feature of Kirby's history is its place in the development of modern garden archaeology. When the Hall was taken into the care of the Office of Works in 1930, G.H. Chettle, the Inspector of Ancient Monuments, applied the techniques of archaeological investigation to a new field: a seventeenth-century garden. The excavation removed large quantities of spoil, and it is now known that the remains of much of the later seventeenth-century garden were stripped away in order to reveal the earlier one. Despite this, the 1930s archaeologists established the form of the early garden with considerable accuracy, and laid it out anew although with concrete kerbs and modern rose bushes.

In the 1980s this garden was considered to be rather misleading because it appeared earlier in date than the house in its current form. Another excavation, carried out in conjunction with research into the extensive Hatton family correspondence, revealed more of the later history of the garden. The recreation of the 1690s parterre, based on a similar contemporary design from Longleat House, Wiltshire, was completed in 1997.

Above: The gardens as laid out with rosebeds before the recreation of the 1690s parterre

Left: Laying out the parterre in grass and gravel in 1994

Right: Detail from a portrait of Anne Hatton, Countess of Winchilsea, attributed to Jonathan Richardson

Mid-nineteenth-century watercolour of Kirby Hall by Thomas Allen

last long. In the following century the gardens fell into decay, although some of the fruit trees still remained in the middle of a field according to nineteenth-century visitors' reports.

The eighteenth century

When Hatton (IV) died in 1706, Kirby fell into decline. Both his sons died childless, and the house passed to the descendants of his daughter by his first wife, who had been saved from the explosion in Guernsey and had later married the 7th Earl of Winchilsea. They took the name Hatton in addition to their own family name, Finch. The main home of Edward Finch-Hatton (d. 1771) was Eastwell Park in Kent, but his son George Finch-Hatton (1747–1823) did not abandon Kirby. Despite a great sale of the contents in 1772, the writer

Horace Walpole described how he heard a rumour in 1786 that George planned 'to refit Kirby, and inhabit it'. Many of the features that remain in the roofed parts of Kirby date from this period, and, when another sale was held in 1824, some of the items were relatively up-to-date furnishings in fashionable materials such as rosewood and bamboo. Some work was carried out on the gardens in the eighteenth century: the stream was dammed to form two lakes, and a bridge (now destroyed) was built.

'That great lonely house'

In 1828 the historian John Nichols wrote that Kirby was 'now dismantled and going fast to decay, the furniture, including a fine collection of pictures, statues, &c. having been sold'. Lady Constance, a member of the family, wrote that her grandfather, the 9th Earl, finally left in 1836 and that the house was then occupied by the earl's agent, later a farmer 'and now a labourer lives in the library'. Kirby's state aroused both melancholy and romance in the visitors who began to seek it out, and the Revd Canon James's description was often quoted. He saw 'the very action of decomposition going on, the crumbling stucco of the ceiling feeding the vampire ivy, the tattered tapestry yet hanging on the wall, the picture flapping in its broken frame'.

The 12th Earl of Winchilsea inherited the Hall in 1887, and newspapers announced the next year that he intended 'at least to preserve the ruins' of it. He also found it a suitable, if occasional, use. In 1894 the *Northamptonshire Herald* described a large picnic in the

Two nineteenth-century photographs of the south side of the inner courtyard, from Architecture of the Renaissance in England *(1894) by J. A. Gotch*

Fragment of an 1880s warning notice to vandals from the Earl of Winchilsea's agent, on one of the walls in the Great Withdrawing Chamber

A rare photograph taken before the roof over the service range to the left of the porch collapsed, in which the symmetry of the hall range is much more apparent than today

grounds organised by the earl for a charitable organisation, the Children's Order of Chivalry. Nearly 2,000 children attended, travelling on special trains that ran from London, Boston and Sleaford. The children were presented to Lord and Lady Winchilsea, and then admitted to a bazaar in the ruins of the Hall. Afterwards there was a cricket match and music from the Gretton brass band.

However, the *Northampton Independent* announced in 1913 that Kirby Hall was for sale. Their columnist was full of melancholic appreciation: 'now, where the courtiers trod a graceful measure grass grows and the bat flits unhindered ... the splendid gardens – adjudged the finest in England – have vanished and are covered in turf; and for days together no one goes to that great lonely house which once resounded with revelry and throbbed with life'. There was still no difficulty in visiting the Hall, though, for in 1918 the cyclist Herbert Evans found that 'the shepherd and his family who tenant one corner of the huge mansion will give you a cordial welcome'. The next year the remaining fittings were removed.

e earnestly requ...
...RE any part of ...
to DEFACE them ...
or W...ting their Names
...on found doing so a...
...ILL BE PROSECUTED.
JNO. ROOKE,
Agent to the Earl of Winchilsea and Nottingham.
8th July, 188.

Rescue

In 1930 the Office of Works took over the management of the property. The Ancient Monuments Branch excavated and restored the garden in the 1930s and installed the estate's former shepherd and his wife as custodians, along with their Alsatian puppies and a cat. Despite the alleged complaints of the local baker, who had to get out of his van six times to open the gates when delivering their bread, they remained as custodians until retirement in 1952, doing their cooking on a range installed in the large fireplace in the Library. Much consolidation work was carried out on the fabric of the

Sheep grazing in the forecourt. In 1844 Samuel Carter Hall wrote that at Kirby 'farm-servants sleep surrounded by exquisite carvings; one room ... decorated with a fine old fire-place ... served, at the time of the artist's visit, the purpose of a dog-kennel'

One of the peacocks at Kirby Hall

View of the top of the south side of the forecourt, from outside the forecourt wall

building from 1930 onwards, always in a spirit of repair rather than reconstruction. In recent years the Hall hosted a festival of historical re-enactment, *History in Action,* and in 1998 some of the rooms were temporarily refurnished as a location for a film adaptation of Jane Austen's *Mansfield Park.*

In 1971 the architectural historian John Summerson eloquently explained the Hall's attraction for him: 'The beauty of Kirby's decline is that it was private and without violence. The house was never burnt, ravaged, used as a quarry or assaulted by mobs. It simply lapsed ... today the masonry is still unsullied, sharp and clear, so that if roofs, windows and doors suddenly reassembled themselves, the stones would take it as an unsurprising compliment'.

This guidebook owes much to the research of Teresa Sladen, Gareth Hughes and especially to the very generous help of Brian Dix, director of the garden excavation of 1987–1994.

Further Reading

Dix, B, Soden, I and Hylton, T 'Kirby Hall and its gardens: excavations in 1987–1994' *Archaeological Journal,* 152, 1995, 291–380.

Summerson, J 'John Thorpe and the Thorpes of Kingscliffe' in *The Unromantic Castle,* 1990.

Heward, J and Taylor, R *The Country Houses of Northampton-shire,* RCHME, 1996.